W9-BHU-876

HANUKKAH TRIVIA

This book is dedicated to Rabbi Robert Waxman
of B'Nai Israel Synagogue, Wilmington, North Carolina,
and with appreciation to Louis Barlow, Rabbi Barry Block,
Arlene Burns, Heidi Fleischer, Catherine Helderman,
Alyson Levy Ray, and Jim Silverberg.

THE ANSWERS BEGIN ON PAGE 77

HANUKKAH
TRIVIA
150 FUN & FASCINATING FACTS ABOUT HANUKKAH

Jennie Miller Helderman & Mary Caulkins

GRAMERCY BOOKS
New York

This 2002 edition is published by Gramercy Books, an imprint of Random House Value Publishing, Inc., 280 Park Avenue, New York, NY 10017, by arrangement with Crane Hill Publishers, Birmingham, Alabama

Gramercy is a registered trademark and the colophon is a trademark of Random House, Inc.

Printed in Singapore

Random House
New York • Toronto • London • Sydney • Auckland
www.randomhouse.com

A catalog record for this title is available from the Library of Congress

ISBN: 0-517-22071-7

9 8 7 6 5 4 3 2 1

Hanukkah is a midwinter Jewish holiday. In 165 B.C. a small army of devout Jews known as the Maccabees rebelled against their Greek-Syrian rulers, eventually overcoming them. The holiday commemorates the rededication of the temple in Jerusalem after it was defiled. Legend says there was only enough pure oil to light the lamps for one night, but through a miracle, the lamps burned for eight days. Since that time, Jews have celebrated Hanukkah by burning lights for eight nights. Hanukkah is also known as the Festival of Lights, the Festival of Dedication, and the Feast of the Maccabees.

1. What is the right way to spell Hanukkah?
   a. Hannukkah, Hannukka, Hannuka
   b. Channuka, Channukah, Chanuka
   c. Hannukah, Hanukkah, Khanukah
   d. Take your pick!

2. Hanukkah is the most historically documented of the Jewish holidays. Where in the Hebrew Bible is the story found?
   a. Numbers
   b. Deuteronomy
   c. Behind the advertisement for the Hunan Garden restaurant
   d. It is not in the Hebrew Bible.

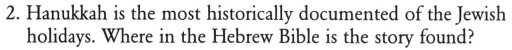

3. What is the Apocrypha?
   a. The story of four horsemen
   b. A Greek translation of biblical-era Hebrew writings
   c. The Dead Sea Scrolls
   d. A floor wax AND a dessert topping!

4. Where in the New Testament is Hanukkah mentioned?

5. While Hanukkah is not recorded in the Hebrew Bible, what biblical prophet foretold the historic events?
   a. Amos
   b. Andy
   c. Hosea
   d. Daniel

6. Where does the name Hanukkah first appear?
    a. The Books of Maccabees
    b. The Talmud
    c. Encyclopedia Judaica
    d. In the sky next to "Surrender Dorothy"

7. How did the Greeks get involved with Hanukkah?
    a. Alexander the Great conquered much of the known world, including Judea.
    b. The Greeks conquered Judea in the Trojan War.
    c. Hercules wrestled with Goliath and won.
    d. Solomon married the Queen of Sheba, whose lineage was Greek.

8. Alexander the Great permitted Jews to continue to observe their religion. What did Simon the Just, the Jewish high priest, promise in return?

a. That he would build a giant statue to span the harbor
b. That ouzo would be served at all festivals
c. That all baby boys born that year would be named Alexander
d. That he would meet a pieman coming down the lane

9. In the years following Alexander's death, many Jews embraced the Greek customs, language, and ideas. These people were known as whom?

a. Trojans
b. Hellenists
c. Grecophiles
d. Wise men

10. The Maccabees rebelled against their rulers, the Greek-Syrians. According to tradition, from which biblical figure does the lineage of Greece descend?

a. Methuselah
b. Noah
c. Ezekiel
d. Alexander the Great

11. Antiochus IV, the Greek-Syrian ruler, called himself Antiochus
    Epiphanes. What does this name mean, and what did the Jews
    call him?
    a. The man from Ephesus, "the profane"
    b. God manifest, "the madman"
    c. The mighty, "the evildoer"
    d. King of Clubs, "the royal flush"

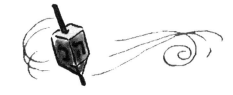

12. As citizens under Antiochus, the Jews willingly paid taxes and served in the army. Antiochus enraged them by banning circumcision, the study of the Torah, and the observance of the Sabbath, under penalty of death. Antiochus also enraged them by constructing:

a. Jacob's ladder
b. The Tower of Babel
c. Statues of himself and the Greek god Zeus
d. Statues of Mars, the Greek god of war, made entirely of feta cheese

13. What wedding custom did Antiochus mandate?
    a. All party napkins must include his name.
    b. He would not allow wine at the wedding feast.
    c. He claimed the privilege of the first night with the bride.
    d. He required pork to be served at the feast.

14. An elderly priest in the little town of Modi'in northwest of Jerusalem began a revolt in 168 B.C. when he refused to obey the demands of Antiochus IV. The priest killed a royal officer and a Jew who complied with the demands. What was the name of the priest?
    a. Mattathias
    b. Judas
    c. Eleazar
    d. Solomon

15. Judas is known as Judas Maccabee because Maccabee means:
    a. He was sponsored by the Maccabee Athletic
       Shoe Company.
    b. Maccabee was the village where Judas was born.
    c. The lion
    d. The hammer

16. Who were the brothers of Judas Maccabee?
    a. Jonathan, Simon, Eleazar, and Johanon
    b. Myron, Marvin, Moses, and Mel
    c. Uriah, Jacob, Joshua, and Joseph
    d. Cain and Abel

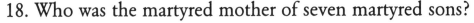

17. According to legend, who was the sister of Judas and what did she do at her wedding?

    a. Bathsheba seduced David.
    b. Hannah stripped naked.
    c. Uhura called starfleet command.
    d. Salome danced wearing seven veils.

18. Who was the martyred mother of seven martyred sons?

    a. Roseanne
    b. Hannah
    c. Judith
    d. Marjorie Morningstar

19. What was the rallying cry of Mattithias as he and his followers fled to the mountains?

a. "Don't shoot until you see the whites of their eyes!"

b. "Praise the Lord and pass the ammunition!"

c. "Who is for the Lord, follow me!"

d. "The Lord's name be praised!"

20. What animal was part of the army in the war of independence fought by the Maccabees?

a. Warrior elephants

b. Spitting camels

c. Tamed tigers

d. Attack dogs

21. The Syrians had the latest weapons: ballistas for throwing stones, battering rams, javelins, spears, swords, bows, and metal armor. What were the weapons used by the Maccabees?
   a. Sticks and stones
   b. The jaws of an ass
   c. Knives and swords
   d. Tiny drink umbrellas

22. Judas and his men recaptured the temple at Jerusalem, cleansed it, and rededicated it on the 25th day of the Hebrew month of Kislev. When did Antiochus defile it?

23. Why did Judas put a wreath on the front door of the temple for its rededication?
    a. The first temple had a wreath on its door.
    b. He got a good buy at a Kmart after-Christmas sale.
    c. It had to do with Hellenism and Sukkot.
    d. The wreath was a symbol of peace.

24. According to the Hebrew Bible, what else happened in the last days of Kislev?
    a. The rain stopped and a rainbow appeared after the biblical flood.
    b. Cain killed Abel, and Moses completed the construction of the temple.
    c. God created Eve, and David slew Goliath.
    d. Miriam placed Moses in the bulrushes, and the walls fell at Jericho.

25. What other Jewish holiday falls on the
    25th of a month?
    a. Rosh Hashanah
    b. Passover
    c. Macy's annual Christmas sale
    d. There are none.

26. Hanukkah is called the Feast of Lights, but even the first-century
    Jewish historian Josephus is uncertain of the origin of this
    name. Some scholars think the name may be derived from:
    a. Phosphorescence in the desert sands
    b. Halley's comet
    c. A prophecy of the coming of Liberace
    d. Beeswax candles from the land of milk and honey

27. In the story of Hanukkah, one cruse of pure oil was discovered. The amount was barely enough to burn for one night, but it miraculously kept the lights burning eight days. What was this miraculous oil?

    a. Cod liver oil
    b. Olive oil
    c. Crisco
    d. Oil of OyVey

28. In biblical times, pure oil was used for:

    a. Anointing kings
    b. The menorah in the temple
    c. Bath oil and perfume for rich people
    d. All of the above

29. Green olives just ripe enough to turn black have the purest oil. How is pure oil extracted?

    a. The olives are lightly beaten to make the oil ooze out.
    b. The olives are crushed between huge stones.
    c. The olives are rubbed with large Stridex pads.
    d. Women stomp on the olives with their feet.

30. Judas Maccabee was killed when an arrow pierced his armor during battle in 160 B.C. How was his younger brother Johanon killed?

    a. He was hurled over the temple by a ballista.
    b. He was poisoned by a traitorous woman.
    c. He was crushed by an elephant.
    d. He was hanged as a spy.

31. The Hasmonean period, which lasted twenty-five years, was the last era of Jewish independence until when?
    a. The death of Julius Caesar
    b. The Ottoman Empire
    c. The opening of the Carnegie Deli in New York City
    d. 1948

32. Who killed off the Hasmonean line?
    a. Alexander the Great
    b. Julius Caesar
    c. Herod
    d. Carlton, the doorman

33. What was the Jewish Supreme Court called?
    a. Sanhedrin
    b. Tippihedron
    c. Sansouci
    d. Sandes Tin

34. Aaron occasionally appears on Hanukkah lamps because he reportedly lit the first Tabernacle menorah. Who was Aaron?
    a. The brother of Moses
    b. Hank's cousin
    c. The son of Mattithias
    d. The father of Elijah

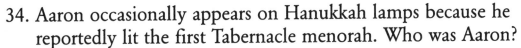

35. Hanukkah lamps are also called:
   a. Menorahs
   b. Hanukkiah
   c. Both of the above
   d. Those lighty thingies

36. What is the proper shape for Hanukkah lamps?
   a. Star-shaped
   b. Circular
   c. All lights in a line
   d. All of the above

37. A democratic vote in the first century A.D. resolved a debate between followers of Hillel and Shammai about whether to light one lamp the first night and increase each night until eight lamps were lit, or to light all eight the first night and decrease the number on following nights. Who won the vote?

38. Why is one light taller than the others on some Hanukkah lamps?
    a. It is the most important.
    b. It is the helper.
    c. It is glad to see you.
    d. All of the above.

39. Who kindles the lights?
    a. The oldest man present
    b. Only women
    c. Children over six
    d. All family members

40. When are the lights kindled?
    a. When the moon is in its seventh hour
       and Jupiter aligns with Mars
    b. When three stars appear
    c. When the moon appears
    d. None of the above

41. When are the lights kindled in the daytime?

42. Hanukkah lights are usually placed outside by a door or in a window. Why is this?
   a. Because of fire ordinances
   b. So Elijah can see to come in
   c. To publicize the miracle
   d. To illuminate the kids's first-semester report cards posted nearby

43. How long should the lights burn?
   a. Until fifty minutes after sunset
   b. For thirty minutes after the first stars appear
   c. Either of the above, depending on when they are lit
   d. Until each family member has eaten eighteen latkes

44. Who is allowed to refrain from work during Hanukkah, and when is this allowed?
    a. Women, while the menorah lights are burning
    b. Men, from sunset to sunup
    c. Elders, for the entire eight days
    d. Lawyers, unless their clients offer to pay in cash

45. How many candles are burned during Hanukkah?
    a. Nine
    b. Forty-four
    c. Seventy-two
    d. Depends on how many your toddler eats

46. Why was the kindling of Hanukkah lights prohibited in Persia during the third century A.D.?
    a. They were a fire hazard because of all the rugs.
    b. There was a shortage of oil.
    c. The Persian governor prohibited all Jewish festivals.
    d. Fire was sacred to the magicians who were in power.

47. In Israel, when do cities close their offices, shops, and public transportation in preparation for Hanukkah?

48. What shape of Hanukkah lamps became popular in nineteenth-century Europe?
    a. Lamps shaped as sofas and chairs
    b. Lamps shaped like Mickey Mouse
    c. Globe-shaped lamps filled with "snow"
    d. Shapes not mentioned

49. In what order are the lights placed in the Hanukkah lamp and kindled?

    a. Placed right to left; kindled right to left
    b. Placed right to left; kindled left to right
    c. Placed left to right; kindled left to right
    d. Placed left to right; kindled right to left

50. "A Song at the Dedication of the House" is recited after the lights are kindled. Who wrote it?

    a. The Bee Gees
    b. The heavenly hosts
    c. Gabriel
    d. David

51. *"Maoz Tzur,"* or "Rock of Ages," is the song usually sung following the lighting of the lamps. Who wrote it?
    a. Rodgers and Hammerstein
    b. Simon and Garfunkel
    c. Mordecai
    d. David

52. A dreidel is a spinning top used in a game at Hanukkah. Hebrew letters on all four sides represent the words *nes gadol hayah sham.* What does this phrase mean?
    a. None, some, half, all
    b. A great miracle happened there.
    c. "Rock of Ages"
    d. Never eat Shredded Wheat.

53. To what place do the words, *nes gadol hayah poh* on a dreidel refer?

    a. Israel
    b. Brighton Beach
    c. Babylon
    d. Baghdad

54. The player who spins *heh* during the dreidel game does what?

    a. Says "Hit me"
    b. Takes half the pot
    c. Antes up
    d. Takes his marbles and goes home

55. What is outstanding about the dreidel at the shopping mall in Cedarhurst, Long Island, near the John F. Kennedy Airport?
    a. It is a hot-air balloon.
    b. It demonstrates perpetual motion.
    c. It is fourteen feet tall.
    d. All of the above

56. Games have long been pastimes for long winter evenings during Hanukkah. Besides the dreidel and cards, what other game has been popular throughout the history of Hanukkah?
    a. Bridge
    b. Parcheesi
    c. Trivial Pursuit
    d. Chess

57. Riddles, as well as word and number games, invented for Hanukkah are called *katowes,* or jests. They are based on the Hebrew system of defining words by the numerical value of their Hebrew letters. What is the answer to all of them?

a. Forty-four
b. Meshuganah
c. Crazy Eights
d. Eight

58. What is the origin of eating cheese at Hanukkah?

a. The Maccabees made cheese from goat milk to survive the siege.
b. Cheese symbolizes long life and happiness.
c. Judith fed cheese to Holofernes to make him thirsty.
d. Eating cheese is forbidden at Hanukkah.

59. What is *sufganiyot?*
    a. Potato pancakes
    b. Jelly doughnuts without the hole
    c. Chopped liver
    d. Pickled herring

60. Latkes are eaten on Hanukkah because:
    a. The Maccabean women threw potatoes at the enemy.
    b. The custom was promoted by Irish Jews.
    c. Latkes are cooked in oil.
    d. Latkes were the favorite food of Judas Maccabee.

61. Other foods traditionally eaten at Hanukkah include:
    a. *Stifatho, puchero,* and lentil pilaf
    b. Roast goose stuffed with apples
    c. Both of the above
    d. Pez candy

62. Where did the most distant celebration
    of Hanukkah take place?
    a. The Russian space station Mir
    b. The NASA space shuttle *Endeavor*
    c. Outer space
    d. All of the above

63. In 1865 the head of Reform Judaism in the United States suggested the elimination of Hanukkah lights. Why was a resolution introduced six years later, urging the celebration of Hanukkah?

a. Jewish families missed it.

b. Jewish families wanted to counteract the celebration of Christmas.

c. Lighting candles turns attention away from greasy latkes in the stomach.

d. The Union of American Hebrew Congregations invested heavily in wax futures.

64. Huge billboards in Rio de Janeiro, Brazil, proclaimed the miracle of lights in 1996. The largest party was held at Club Entro Adolfo Bloch. What was the featured food at the party?
    a. Kosher sushi
    b. Latkes with salsa
    c. Black beans and rice
    d. Zayerah pickles with bagels

65. What is the origin of Hanukkah *gelt*, or the custom of giving money to children?
    a. Bribery
    b. Education
    c. Santa Claus
    d. Lowering taxable income

66. What United States Supreme Court case impacted the public observance of Hanukkah?
    a. *Wally World Theme Parks, Inc. v. Clark Griswold*
    b. *Goldberg v. Frankfurter*
    c. *County of Allegheny v. ACLU*
    d. *ACLU v. Skokie*

67. How did Jewish residents of the Venice, Italy, ghetto during the Middle Ages observe Hanukkah?
    a. They held a wine-spitting contest.
    b. They rode in gondolas through the canals looking for menorahs.
    c. They put garlic in their latkes.
    d. They danced a circle dance in the Piazza de San Marco.

68. Why has the fifth night of Hanukkah in Israel been called "The Black Fifth Night?"
    a. To commemorate the throwing of the World Series by the White Sox in 1919
    b. To remember the death of Judas Maccabee in 160 B.C.
    c. To recall the night the world's largest menorah fell
    d. To remember when the Turks expelled all Jews from Tel Aviv and Jaffa during World War I

69. According to Philip R. Alstat's short story, "Lights Are Kindled in Bergen-Belsen," what did the Jews in the concentration camp use for a candle during their secret Hanukkah ceremony in 1943?

70. What popular American folk singer wrote and sang the
Hanukkah song, "Light One Candle?"

a. Peter Yarrow
b. Carly Simon
c. Phil Ochs
d. Bob Dylan

71. In 1995, archaeologists working at a site thirty kilometers
northwest of Jerusalem found twenty-three ossuaries, or stone
boxes, in a cave. What did they contain?

a. Menorahs
b. Petrified latkes
c. Powerball lottery tickets
d. Bones

72. Which significant archaeological discovery was made in 1998?
    a. Noah's ark
    b. The world's oldest synagogue
    c. Calgon really is an ancient Chinese secret.
    d. The ark of the covenant

73. What was in line, online, pressure sensitive, and new in 1997?
    a. The Doodle family
    b. Hanukkah seals
    c. MacHannu.com graphics
    d. MacHannu Internet stock

74. What new gourmet soda hit the market for Hanukkah in 1998?
    a. Dreideljuice
    b. Candle Lite
    c. Gefiltefizz
    d. Maccacola

75. The Falashas claim to be descendants of King Solomon and the Queen of Sheba. They observe all Jewish festivals except Hanukkah. Where are they from?
    a. A galaxy far, far away
    b. Ethiopia
    c. Falafel
    d. Egypt

76. Which NFL offensive line played with dreidels during Hanukkah in 1998?

   a. New York Jets
   b. Kansas City Chiefs
   c. Chicago Bear Markets
   d. Oakland Dreiders

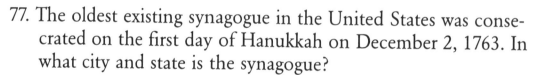

77. The oldest existing synagogue in the United States was consecrated on the first day of Hanukkah on December 2, 1763. In what city and state is the synagogue?

   a. Newport, Rhode Island
   b. Savannah, Georgia
   c. Philadelphia, Pennsylvania
   d. Boston, Massachusetts

78. Which were advertised in the Yiddish press during the 1920s as perfect gifts for Hanukkah?
    a. Hudson motorcars
    b. Colgate dental creme
    c. Aunt Jemima pancake flour and Crisco shortening
    d. All of the above

79. What did the East River Savings Institution advertise in 1925?
    a. Hanukkah toasters
    b. A Christmas savings plan
    c. Free chocolate *gelt*
    d. Savings banks shaped like dreidels

80. In its *Der Tog* ad, what did the Libby Hotel Corporation claim made the "nicest Chanukah present?"
    a. An eight-day holiday visit
    b. Menorahs shaped like the hotels
    c. Stock in the corporation
    d. Stolen hotel towels

81. In *Mother Goose Rhymes for Jewish Children,* which was among the earliest Jewish children's books, who came for Hanukkah?
    a. Dick and Jane
    b. Shlomo, the out-of-work moyel
    c. Aunt Mollie
    d. Mrs. Goldberg

82. What was unusual about the menorah offered by a leading manufacturer of Jewish ritual products in the 1940s?
    a. It was a musical menorah made of chrome.
    b. Marc Chagall designed the menorah.
    c. The menorah was made of kosher chocolate.
    d. People were urged to buy five and get a mah-jongg set as a gift.

83. What was the "Barton's Race Dredel?"
    a. The lead-out at Ballyhoo
    b. An Israelized version of the game of Monopoly
    c. A play in Yiddish theater
    d. A Jewish pinball game

84. What was Barton's offer for Hanukkah in 1951?

85. Loft's Chocolates made a spinwheel game in the 1940s called Valor Against Oppression. Who was one of its latter-day Maccabees?
   a. Amadeo Modigliani
   b. Isaac Mizrachi
   c. Hyman G. Rickover
   d. Moshe Dayan

86. When was the first Hanukkah postage stamp issued in the United States?
   a. 1966
   b. 1976
   c. 1986
   d. 1996

87. What American writer wrote a five-act Hanukkah drama?
   a. Al Franken
   b. Herman Wouk
   c. Henry Wadsworth Longfellow
   d. Isaac Bashevis Singer

88. What famous composer wrote an oratorio called *Judas Maccabeus?*
    a. Handel
    b. Mozart
    c. Bach
    d. Weird Al Yankovich

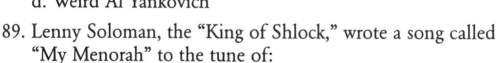

89. Lenny Soloman, the "King of Shlock," wrote a song called "My Menorah" to the tune of:
    a. "My Sharona" by The Knack
    b. "La Bamba" by Ritchie Valens
    c. "Blue Christmas" by Elvis Presley
    d. "My Way" by Frank Sinatra

90. Where in 1998 was Hanukkah celebrated publicly for the first time in more than five hundred years?
    a. Russia
    b. Spain
    c. Argentina
    d. New Jersey

91. In the Rugrats Hanukkah television special, Tommy's motto was:
    a. "Let's get dangerous."
    b. "A Macababy's got to do what a Macababy's got to do."
    c. "Pancakes-Shmancakes – Let's eat!"
    d. "All for one, but more for me."

92. What does Tommy call Hanukkah?
    a. Harmonica
    b. Veronica
    c. Santa Monica
    d. High Colonica

93. What does Stu, the inventor, make for the end of the Hanukkah play in the Rugrats Hanukkah television special?
    a. A Judah Maccabee doll
    b. A latke machine
    c. A dreidel computer game
    d. A menorah

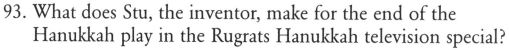

94. What does Grandpa Boris say is the miracle of Hanukkah in the Rugrats Hanukkah television special?
    a. That Rudolph the Red-Nosed Reindeer doesn't light the way
    b. That, at his age, he can stay awake through the celebration
    c. That fried latkes have clogged his people's arteries for two thousand years, yet they still survive
    d. That he won the dreidel game

95. *Saturday Night Live* aired a sketch in 1989 that included the character, Hanukkah Harry. Who played Hanukkah Harry?
    a. Dana Carvey
    b. The ghost of John Belushi
    c. Jon Lovitz
    d. Phil Hartman

96. What did Hanukkah Harry do in the sketch?
    a. Stole presents from the rich and gave them to the poor
    b. Sang to all the good little Jewish boys and girls
    c. Saved Christmas
    d. Made up a new dance for the Hanukkah celebration

97. What did Hanukkah Harry use to deliver the gifts?
    a. A sled pulled by three elephants
    b. A train car pulled by three crocodiles
    c. A motorcycle pulled by four goats
    d. A wagon pulled by three donkeys

98. What were the names of Hanukkah Harry's donkeys?
    a. Moshe, Herschel, and Shlomo
    b. Moe, Larry, and Curly
    c. Groucho, Harpo, and Chico
    d. Hortense, Abraham, and Sidney

99. What gift or gifts did Hanukkah Harry leave?
    a. Eight pairs of socks, slacks that are too big,
       a dreidel, and chocolate coins
    b. His Hanukkah video
    c. Long underwear, earmuffs, Limburger cheese,
       and doughnuts
    d. A new Cadillac and an all-expenses-paid trip to New Jersey

100. *Northern Exposure* aired on CBS from 1990 to 1995. In a 1991 episode during Hanukkah, Dr. Joel Fleischman gets his first Christmas tree. Who helped him decorate it, and what were the decorations?

   a. Maggie O'Connell; raven lights and ornaments
   b. Ed Chigliak; strung popcorn and candles
   c. Ruth-Anne Miller; tin stars
   d. Maurice Minnifield; white lights and wine labels

101. What does Anne Frank's father plan for a Hanukkah gift in *The Diary of Anne Frank, The Critical Edition?*

   a. A new diary
   b. A dreidel
   c. Photos of her favorite movie stars
   d. A New Testament Bible

102. In the play, *The Diary of Anne Frank,* what does Anne give
Margot for Hanukkah?
a. A scarf
b. Shampoo
c. A crossword puzzle book
d. Earplugs

103. What World War I officer led victorious Allied forces into
Jerusalem on the first day of Hanukkah in 1917?
a. Capt. Hawkeye Pierce
b. Lord Allenby, a British military leader
c. Moshe Dayan
d. Col. Mickey Marcus

104. What is the opening scene in the Broadway play, *The Last Night of Ballyhoo?*
    a. Reba lighting the Hanukkah candles
    b. Sunny and Peachy Weil playing the dreidel game
    c. Lala decorating a Christmas tree
    d. Miss Daisy driving to the synagogue

105. What figure associated with Hanukkah has inspired more writers, musicians, and artists than any other character in the Apocrypha?

106. How often will there be a new moon on the first day of Hanukkah?

107. What do the Hebrew letters mean in the holiday's name?

108. "Judah Maccabee" is a song about the history of Hanukkah. Who wrote it?
     a. Rabbi Joe Black
     b. Isaac Stern
     c. Ernest Bloch
     d. Saul Tschernichovsky

109. Who popularized "Hanukkah Rock?"
     a. The Dew Drop Dreidel Spinners
     b. Rabbi R. Waxman and the Simcha Players
     c. Gefilte Joe and the Fish
     d. The Melvin Kaminsky Band

110. Who wrote "The Chanukah Song" for his album, which hit the top of the charts?
    a. Irving Berlin
    b. Elvis
    c. Sammy Davis, Jr.
    d. Kenny G

111. According to the song "Soufganiot," these jelly doughnuts are:
    a. Full of cholesterol
    b. Fat-free
    c. In three flavors – raspberry, strawberry, and chocolate
    d. All of the above

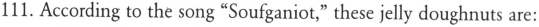

112. What is tall and decked in blue-and-white lights the night before Hanukkah?

a. The conch at Key West
b. The Washington Monument
c. The Eiffel Tower
d. The Empire State Building

113. How did Jewish and Texan traditions mix in 1997?

114. Where did the people of Bilgoray celebrate the last night of Hanukkah in Isaac Bashevis Singer's story, "The Extinguished Lights"?

a. Before Reb Berish's fireplace
b. At the new synagogue
c. In the cemetery
d. None of the above

115. Isaac Bashevis Singer wrote about Dreidel. Who or what was Dreidel?
   a. The man who designed a Jewish version of the game Monopoly
   b. A child who liked to spin in circles
   c. A yellow-green parakeet
   d. A song written by Singer's grandmother

116. How did the Polish squire lose his money in Isaac Bashevis Singer's story, "The Squire"?
   a. Playing dreidel with Falik's children
   b. Gambling at the horse races
   c. Through a hole in the pocket of his gray silk pants
   d. It was baked in a pie.

117. Where was Hanukkah celebrated for the first time ever in 1997?
    a. The Capitol in Washington, D.C.
    b. Mecca
    c. The Vatican
    d. Katmandu

118. The Italian government officially held a Hanukkah ceremony in 1997 at Rome's Arch of Titus. What was the significance of the location?
    a. It is where the Maccabees signed the peace treaty.
    b. It is the part of Rome built in one day.
    c. It was the site of the first McDonald's in Italy and was renamed the Golden Arch of Titus.
    d. It was built to celebrate the sack of Jerusalem in A.D. 70.

119. More than thirty world leaders participated in ceremonies opening Hanukkah on December 23, 1997. Other than Hanukkah, what was the occasion?

a. One thousand years since the last dedication of the Temple
b. The United Nations World Day of Peace
c. Israel's fiftieth anniversary
d. Israel's bicentennial

120. What makes Hanukkah and Purim different from the other Jewish holidays?

121. Who said, "Had Antiochus succeeded in obliterating Jewry a century and a half before the birth of Jesus, there would have been no Christmas. The Feast of the Nativity rests on the victory of Hanukkah?"
    a. Billy Graham
    b. Herman Wouk
    c. Martin Luther King
    d. Isaac Asimov

122. Whom does Adam Sandler identify as being Jewish in "The Hanukkah Song?"
    a. Ann Landers and Dear Abby
    b. Kirk Douglas and Dinah Shore
    c. Capt. Kirk and Mr. Spock
    d. All of the above

123. What did Steuben design for the 1996 Hanukkah season?

124. What 1994 Hanukkah gift made a whirring noise?

125. When was the first Hanukkah menorah kindled on the Ellipse in Washington, D.C., and who was president of the United States at that time?

a. 1948, Harry Truman
b. 1919, Woodrow Wilson
c. 1978, Jimmy Carter
d. 1996, Bill Clinton

126. Where is the world's largest Hanukkah menorah?
    a. Jerusalem
    b. New York
    c. Philadelphia
    d. Miami

127. Where is Hanukkah celebrated with a relay race in which participants carry torches?
    a. Miami Beach, Florida
    b. Modi'in, Israel
    c. Nafplio, Greece
    d. Stockholm, Sweden

128. Olivia Goldsmith, bestselling author of *The First Wives Club*, includes a Hanukkah scene in her recent book, *Marrying Mom*. What does Phyllis Geronomous buy for herself on the last day of Hanukkah?
    a. A diamond necklace
    b. An insurance policy
    c. A gold Cadillac convertible
    d. Silk lingerie

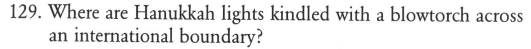

129. Where are Hanukkah lights kindled with a blowtorch across an international boundary?

130. What is the Dreidel House?

    a. A museum for antique dreidels

    b. A homeless shelter

    c. A hut where kids can meet a costumed Judas Maccabee

    d. A public relations firm specializing in spin

131. What is a *Maccabiah?*

    a. An international Jewish Olympics event held in Israel

    b. A musical instrument

    c. The Jewish version of the Pillsbury Bake-off

    d. A macaroni pie

132. How many candles are lit during the eight
nights of Hanukkah if none are lit twice?
a. Eight
b. Thirty-six
c. Forty-four
d. Sixty-four

133. Who were the special guests at the Gothenburg, Sweden,
Hanukkah menorah lighting in 1996?
a. Bjorn Borg and his family
b. Anita Ekberg and her husband
c. Raoul Wallenberg's family
d. Batman and Robin

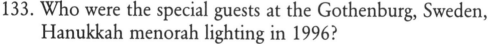

134. Which general was so inspired by a set of Hanukkah lights that after the war he presented its owner with a gold coin engraved with a Hanukkah menorah?
    a. Dwight Eisenhower
    b. Napoleon
    c. George Washington
    d. Robert E. Lee

135. In Kurdistan during Hanukkah, children carry dolls of Antiochus IV and ask for money. What do they do at the end of the day?
    a. Buy doughnuts with the money
    b. Set fire to the dolls
    c. Add the money to the dreidel pot
    d. Buy candles for the poor

136. Why is the fifth night of Hanukkah special in Eastern Europe?

137. In the short story "Hanukkah at Valley Forge" by Emily Solis-Cohen, a boy named Judah travels all day to take something to his father, who was in George Washington's army. What did he take?

a. Food
b. A dreidel
c. A menorah
d. A gun

138. Sadie R. Weilerstein's story, "How Ruth Went Out at Night," is about a little girl who:

    a. Bundles up to see the Hanukkah lights in her neighborhood

    b. Goes out with her friends to sing Hanukkah songs

    c. Takes jelly doughnuts to old people from her synagogue

    d. Goes to her grandmother's to learn how to make latkes

139. What popular Hanukkah story is told in the second act of Henry Wadsworth Longfellow's *Judah Maccabeus*?

    a. The story of Hannah and her seven sons

    b. The story of the dreidel

    c. The miracle of the oil

    d. The story of Judith

140. What historical novelist wrote the prize-winning *My Glorious Brothers,* about the Maccabean revolt?

    a. Howard Fast
    b. Charlotte Brontë
    c. Saul Bellow
    d. Ernest Hemingway

141. In Chaim Potok's short story, "Miracles for a Broken Planet," his family's 1938 Hanukkah celebration is almost ruined because:

    a. The oil for the menorah runs out.
    b. The neighbors are singing their Christmas carols too loudly.
    c. In Germany a Jewish boy shot and killed a German.
    d. His father is in a bad mood.

142. What Jewish festival besides Hanukkah is mentioned in
   The Diary of Anne Frank?

   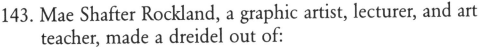

   a. Passover
   b. Yom Kippur
   c. Shevuot
   d. None

143. Mae Shafter Rockland, a graphic artist, lecturer, and art
   teacher, made a dreidel out of:

   a. Broccoli
   b. Recycled denim
   c. Recycled plastic
   d. Potato chips

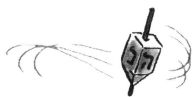

144. The "camp" looking menorah made by Mae Shafter Rockland uses a famous American symbol as the candle holders. What is this symbol?
    a. The yellow smiley face
    b. The American flag
    c. Statues of George Washington
    d. The Statue of Liberty

145. What words are printed around the bottom of Mae Shafter Rockland's menorah?
    a. "Come on Baby Light My Fire"
    b. Patrick Henry's speech, "Give Me Liberty or Give Me Death"
    c. Emma Lazarus's poem, "The New Colossus"
    d. The lyrics to Lenny Soloman's song, "My Menora"

146. The 1994 children's Hanukkah gift, Doodle Dreidel, did what?
a. It spit out blue and white jelly beans.
b. It made the "cock-a-doodle-doo" noise of a rooster as it spun.
c. It created art.
d. It floated so children could play with it in the bathtub.

147. The British Museum in London contains the world's largest collection of what from the Maccabean period?
a. Ancient Maccabean coins
b. Menorahs
c. Art depicting the Maccabean revolt
d. Olive oil

148. One of the most symbolic objects associated with Hanukkah's celebration is the menorah. According to Exodus, who fashioned the first menorah for the Tabernacle in the desert and what did it look like?

    a. Jethro; it was made of silver and had nine interwoven serpent heads.

    b. Bezalel; it was made of pure gold with seven cups shaped like almond blossoms.

    c. Moses; it had small stone cups for holding the oil.

    d. Moses's daughter; seven tiny powder puffs and one lipstick.

149. What is Zot Hanukkah?

    a. It is the eighth and last day of Hanukkah.

    b. It is a celebration where women read in Old Yiddish about the heroine, Judith.

    c. It means "This Is the Dedication."

    d. All of the above

150. Natan Alterman, the author of the poem, "It Happened on Hanukkah," wrote several volumes of poetry, plays, and children's books. For what else is he known?

    a. He can blow the biggest bubble gum bubble in Israel.

    b. He paints himself blue and white for all poetry recitations.

    c. He was the first person inside the Barney costume.

    d. He is a translator of William Shakespeare's works.

151. Susan Braunstein, curator of Jewish archaeology at the Jewish Museum in Manhattan, boasts the world's largest collection of what?
    a. Statues of Judas Maccabee
    b. Pottery from the Maccabean period
    c. Menorahs
    d. Dust bunnies

152. The Italian Renaissance sculptor Donatello's bronze figures of Judith and Holofernes are in the Palazzo Vecchio in Florence, Italy. What modern fictitious character lurks in their shadow?
    a. Dirk Pitt
    b. Dr. Hannibal Lecter
    c. Jack Ryan
    d. John Jakes

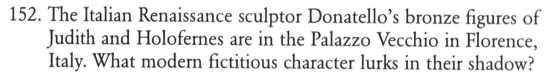

ANSWERS

1. (d) Take your pick! All are attempts to spell in English a word written in the Hebrew alphabet, and no spelling is more correct than another. In Hebrew, Hanukkah requires only five letters.

2. (d) The story of the Maccabees is not found in the Hebrew Bible. The sources for Hanukkah are 1 Maccabees and 2 Maccabees, in the Apocrypha. Sources also include the works of Josephus, a first-century Jewish historian; the Talmud; and a medieval work called The Scroll of Antiochus.

3. (b) A Greek translation of biblical-era Hebrew writings containing fourteen books. These books were not included in the Bible by Jews or Protestants. Roman Catholics accept eleven in their Bible.

4. In John 10:22–23, where Jesus goes to Jerusalem for the Festival of Dedication, or Hanukkah.

5. (d) Daniel. In the eighth chapter of the book of Daniel, the prophet tells of a dream he had about a shaggy goat with a peculiar horn. The angel Gabriel interprets the dream to predict the battles between the Maccabees and the Syrians.

6. (b) The Talmud. The Talmud was written a few hundred years after the Books of Maccabees.

7. (a) Alexander the Great conquered much of the known world, including Judea in the fourth century B.C. Following his death at the age of thirty-three, his empire split apart. After years of struggle among Greek generals, Syria began ruling the land of Israel.

8. (c) That all baby boys born that year would be named Alexander.

9. (b) Hellenists

10. (b) Noah, through his son, Yefet, who had seven sons. Yavan (Greece) was the fourth.

11. (b) God manifest. The Jews called Antiochus "Epimanes," or "the madman." He inherited the Greek-Syrian throne following the untimely death of his older brother. Rumors flourished that Antiochus played a role in his brother's demise.

12. (c) Statues of himself and the Greek god Zeus. Antiochus ordered his soldiers to enforce the decrees and hold ceremonies sacrificing pigs.

13. (c) Jewish brides were told to spend their wedding night with the governor or his officers before going to their husbands. Consequently, the Jews declined to wed for more than three years.

14. (a) Mattithias (or Mattithiah or Matityahu, other spellings), a member of the Hasmonean dynasty. Mattithias, his five sons, and a number of faithful Jews fled into the mountains and began the revolt against the armies of Antiochus. Mattithias died the following year, leaving his third son, Judas, in command.

15. (d) The hammer. Scholars believe that the nickname, "Maccabee," comes from the Hebrew word for hammer, and that it refers the hammer-like tactics Judas used in battle. Others say that hammer refers to the shape of his head. Some say it means "quencher" as in the one who quenched Hellenism. Regardless, the name Maccabee refers to the dynasty that led the revolt. The history of the Maccabees is preserved in four books of the Apocrypha.

16. (a) Jonathan, Simon, Eleazar, and Johanon

17. (b) Hannah. Rather than submitting to the governor on her wedding night, Hannah stripped naked at the wedding feast, shocking the people into avenging the sacrilege and humiliation of the daughters of Israel. Medieval manuscripts include this version of the way the war started.

18. (b) Hannah. Not the sister of Judas Maccabee, but another Hannah whose story is found in 2 Maccabees. One by one, Syrians tortured and killed Hannah's sons because they refused to eat pork. After her sons were killed, Hannah also died. Her martyrdom is the subject of poems and stories recited during Hanukkah for centuries. Hannah and her sons chose death over committing sacrilege.

19. (c) "Who is for the Lord, follow me!" 1 Maccabees 2:27.

20. (b) Warrior elephants. Several dozen elephants, compared to modern day tanks, fought on the losing side.

21. (a) Sticks and stones. The sticks and stones were bound into maces, shepherds' slingshots, and farm implements.

22. The 25th of Kislev, exactly three years earlier.

23. (c) It had to do with Hellenism and Sukkot. According to 1 Maccabees, when Judas and his followers rededicated the temple, they "decked the front of the Temple with crowns of gold and small shields." Crowns in that period were wreaths, Hellenistic symbols of victory, which attested to the Hellenistic influence during that century. Judas also put a wreath on the front door of the temple, because Hanukkah originally was celebrated as a second Sukkot, a fall harvest festival when participants often donned leafy wreaths.

24. (b) Cain killed Abel, and Moses completed the construction of the temple; Bereshit Rabbah 22; Numbers Rabbah 13. On the 27th day of Kislev, the rain stopped and a rainbow appeared after the biblical flood; Genesis 8:3; Rashi..

25. (d) There are none.

26. (b) Halley's comet was due to appear in 163 B.C., although there is some question surrounding the date of its appearance. It is said to have appeared, unusually close to the earth, while the Maccabees were purifying the temple. The comet may have influenced the lighting of lamps on Hanukkah because of its spectacular display in the sky.

27. (b) Olive oil

28. (d) All of the above

29. (a) The olives are lightly beaten to make the oil ooze out. The oil, which is just under the skin, is known as pure or beaten oil. There is more oil in the pulp, but it is not as pure. Olive oil is extracted by crushing olives between two large stones and is used for fuel, cooking, and making soaps, perfumes, and medicines.

30. (c) An elephant crushed him.

31. (d) 1948. The year was the beginning of the modern state of Israel. The end of the Hasmonean period until the formation of the modern state of Israel spanned 1,988 years.

32. (c) Herod. The king of Judea rose to power under the Romans. The historian Josephus records Herod's insane jealousy of all descendants of the Hasmonean line.

33. (a) Sanhedrin. The Jewish Supreme Court also was called the *Beit Din*. The Sanhedrin determined when each new month began based on when a new moon was observed. During months with holidays, the Sanhedrin sent messengers to towns outside Jerusalem so people would know when to celebrate Hanukkah and other holidays.

34. (a) The brother of Moses. Aaron also was a high priest.

35. (c) Both of the above. The *hanukkiah* are special menorahs that have eight candles or oil lamps and one *shammash,* unlike the Temple Menorahs with seven candles. It is forbidden to reproduce the Temple Menorah. Today the word "menorah" is commonly used to mean either one. Lighting the candles is the most visible observance of Hanukkah.

36. (d) All of the above. Lamps in these shapes and others have been used throughout the history of Hanukkah. The shape of the lamp is unimportant, but it is essential that the flames remain separate and not blend as in a pagan bonfire. It was not until the Middle Ages that the *hanukkiah* was used.

37. Hillel. The president of the Sanhedrin suggested lighting one lamp on the first night of Hanukkah, and increasing to eight lamps during the celebration.

38. (b) It is the helper. This light is sometimes called the *shammash* or beadle, and is used to light the other eight candles. These eight lights are holy and are not supposed to be used for illumination or kindling any other flame. All of these lights are on the same level, symbolizing the fact that no single day of Hanukkah is more important than the others.

39. (d) All family members. The age or sex of the family member is unimportant. In fact, each member of the family is allowed to have his own lamp.

40. (b) When three stars appear. However, the lights can be lit any time after sundown. It is preferable to kindle the lights while the household is still awake and people are still on the streets.

41. During war when lights at night would reveal soldiers to their enemies.

42. (c) To publicize the miracle. The lights are placed to the left of the entrance, and opposite from the *mezuzah* (door post) if it is outside.

43. (c) Either of the above. The amount of time the lights burn depends on whether they are lit at sunset or lit when the first stars appear in the sky.

44. (a) Women are allowed to refrain from work while the menorah lights are burning. Work such as laundry and sewing are prohibited, but cooking is permitted.

45. (b) Forty-four

46. (d) Fire was sacred to the magicians who were in power.

47. Hanukkah is not a legal holiday in Israel. Nothing closes, and business goes on as usual.

48. (a) Lamps shaped as sofas and chairs. (Hanukkah lamps in the United States in the twentieth century have taken the other shapes.)

49. (b) Placed right to left; kindled left to right. Just as Hebrew is read from right to left, the lights are placed in the candle right to left. The first candle is placed at the far right on the first night, but the newest light is lit first on the Hanukkah lamp. The light on the far left of the lamp is the first lit each night of the celebration.

50. (d) David. The song is Psalm 30, composed by King David to be sung when his son, Shlomo, dedicated the Temple. Supposedly Judas Maccabee and his followers chanted this song while rededicating the temple in 165 B.C. Sephardim always recite the psalm. Ashkenazim recite it at synagogue services for Hanukkah.

51. (c) Mordecai. Nothing is known about Mordecai except that he wrote the song during the Middle Ages. Mordecai marked his work with an acrostic. The first letter of each line of the song corresponds to the letters of his name. The tune is a medley of a sixteenth-century German church hymn and a folk song.

52. (b) A great miracle happened there.

53. (a) Israel. In Israel, the translation of *nes gadol hayah poh* is: "A great miracle happened here."

54. (b) Takes half the pot. *Nun*, or "N," equals nothing; *gimel*, or "G," takes all the pot; and *shin*, or "S," antes up. The game is usually played with pennies, raisins, nuts, or chocolate-covered "coins."

55. (c) It is fourteen feet tall.

56. (d) Chess. Literary sources, along with early prints and paintings of Hanukkah scenes, show people playing chess.

57. (a) Forty-four, which represents the number of candles burned during Hanukkah. There is even a recipe for a *katowes* cake that has forty-four ingredients.

58. (c) Judith. The beautiful widow fed salty cheese to Holofernes, a general from Asia Minor, to make him thirsty. Then she gave him wine to make him drunk. When he fell asleep in a stupor, she took his sword and cut off his head. After the general's death, his demoralized soldiers fled.

59. (b) Jelly doughnuts without the hole. The doughnuts are fried in oil and often covered with powdered sugar in keeping with an Israeli Hanukkah tradition.

60. (c) Latkes are cooked in oil, referring to the miracle of the oil burning for eight days. Latkes are potato pancakes.

61. (c) Both of the above. Hanukkah foods are seasonal, folkloric, and hearty because Hanukkah is a winter holiday. *Stifatho* in Greece is a beef casserole flavored with cinnamon and saffron. *Puchero* is a South American meat-and-chickpea stew. The tradition of roasting a goose comes from the Dutch, and lentil pilaf is served in India and the Middle East.

62. (d) All of the above. In December 1997, astronaut David Wolf celebrated Hanukkah aboard the Russian space station Mir with a menorah and chocolate candy his sister sent via a Russian supply ship the previous October. Astronaut Jeff Hoffman, the first male Jewish astronaut, also celebrated Hanukkah in space, aboard the shuttle *Endeavor*.

63. (b) Jewish families wanted to counteract the celebration of Christmas.

64. (a) Kosher sushi

65. (b) Education. The Hebrew word *Hanukkah* contains the root word for education, *Hinnuch*. Several centuries ago, Hanukkah was a time for the community to discuss social issues and educational matters. People gave teachers and schools money in appreciation. Eventually, people began giving money to children who answered riddles or questions correctly. Today, the money it is just an outright gift to children.

66. (c) *County of Allegheny v. ACLU* found that a Hanukkah menorah next to a Christmas tree outside Pittsburgh's city-county building was constitutional. The menorah met the "reindeer rule" cited in the 1984 case *Lynch v. Donnelly,* meaning it could not be seen as an endorsement of a religious faith.

67. (b) They rode in gondolas through the canals looking for menorahs. The Jewish residents greeted homeowners who displayed menorahs with a blessing and happy Hanukkah song.

68. (d) To remember when the Turks expelled all Jews from Tel Aviv and Jaffa during World War I.

69. Determined to celebrate Hanukkah and draw strength from the heroic story of the Maccabees, the inmates made a candle from saved bits of fat, a makeshift wick of threads from tattered garments, and a candleholder from half of a raw potato. Dreidels for children were carved out of wooden shoes.

70. (a) Peter Yarrow. The folk singer of Peter, Paul & Mary fame wrote the song after visiting Soviet Jewish refuseniks. For Yarrow, menorah lights became a symbol of the Russian Jewish community's desire to emigrate so they could practice Judaism in a free society.

71. (d) Bones. The boxes were inscribed with the word *Hasmonean* and were the first physical evidence of the existence of the Maccabees. Until this find, the Maccabees were known only through ancient writings.

72. (b) The world's oldest synagogue. The synagogue dates back to the Maccabean period of 50–70 B.C., and was found outside the present West Bank town of Jericho. The synagogue was not lavish, but its floors may have been carpeted. The structure is important because of its age and its direct connection with the Maccabean period. It is an example of synagogues prior to the destruction of the Temple in A.D. 70.

73. (b) Hanukkah seals sponsored by the American Lung Association

74. (c) Gefiltefizz. The drink is a blueberry soda the color of Windex sold for the holiday by Oop! Juice, based in Rhode Island.

75. (b) Ethiopia. Until the seventeenth century, Falashas lived in an independent province in northern Ethiopia. Today nearly all have relocated to Israel.

76. (a) The New York Jets. Right guard Alex Bernstein gave dreidels to his fellow linemen. Matt O'Dwyer explained the significance of the Hebrew letters to them.

77. (a) Newport, Rhode Island. The Touro Synagogue was designed by the colonial architect Peter Harrison and is a national landmark.

78. (d) All of the above, plus waffle irons, Canada Dry ginger ale, and Goodman's noodles were advertised in *Der Tog* and the *Morgen Zhurnal.*

79. (b) A Christmas savings plan. "Save for Chanukah" was the slogan of a December 1925 ad in *Der Tog*. It suggested customers set aside cash through its popular Christmas plan. In Christmas Club Savings Accounts, which began in 1905 and spread to 8,000 banks, depositors saved a small amount each week until two weeks prior to the holiday.

80. (c) Stock in the corporation

81. (c) Aunt Mollie, in *Aunt Mollie Came for Chanukah*. In the book, Aunt Mollie brought toys. Such stories added the stamp of approval to gift-giving at Hanukkah.

82. (a) It was a musical menorah made of chrome. Ziontalis, the manufacturer, created a menorah that played *"Hatikvah"* or "Rock of Ages." It was available in forty-seven different styles and never needed polishing.

83. (b) An Israelized version of Monopoly. The board, which featured a map of Israel, miniature Israeli flags, and menorahs, was created after 1948 by Barton's, a manufacturer of kosher chocolate.

84. Chocolate latkes. A box of fifteen sold for $1.19.

85. (d) Moshe Dayan. Modigliani was an Italian painter and sculptor; Mizrachi is a fashion designer; Rickover was the admiral responsible for the nuclear United States Navy. All are Jewish.

86. (d) 1996. The United States and Israel jointly issued a stamp designed by Hannah Smotrich depicting a colorful menorah, printed for both countries in Clinton, South Carolina. It cost 32 cents in the United States and 2.5 shekel in Israel. The stamp will increase to 33 cents in the United States for Hanukkah 1999. The United States issued 104 million of these stamps.

87. (c) Henry Wadsworth Longfellow wrote "Judah Maccabeus" in 1872 based on the Maccabean victory over the Syrians. The drama formed one division in *The Three Books of Song*, published in 1872.

88. (a) George Frederick Handel presented the oratorio in 1747 at The Royal Opera House in London. There were only five thousand Jews in all of England at that time.

89. (b) "La Bamba" by Ritchie Valens

90. (b) Spain. The Jewish community in Spain celebrated Hanukkah December 20, 1998, in Girona, where their ancestors sought protection in 1391. Their ancestors remained in Girona until they were expelled from Spain in 1492. The ceremony was led by Israel's chief rabbi of Sephardic Jews, who trace their ancestry to Spain.

91. (b) "A Macababy's got to do what a Macababy's got to do." "The Rugrats Hanukkah" was a 1997 production on the Nickelodeon television network.

92. (a) Harmonica

93. (d) A menorah. Stu wants his son and wife to know he's supportive of Hanukkah, so he invents a turbocharged menorah that literally brings down the house.

94. (c) That fried latkes have clogged his people's arteries for two thousand years, yet they still survive.

95. (c) Jon Lovitz

96. (c) Saved Christmas. Santa gets the flu and calls on Harry. Harry is the only other person with magical powers and fills in for Santa.

97. (d) A wagon pulled by three donkeys

98. (a) Moshe, Herschel, and Shlomo

99. (a) Hanukkah Harry leaves eight pairs of socks and a dreidel for the girl, and slacks that are too big and chocolate coins for the boy.

100. (a) Maggie O'Connell; raven lights and ornaments. Fleischman agonizes about being Jewish and his fondness for Christmas trees. After some soul-searching, he gives the tree to Maggie as a gift. The ravens are the symbol for the town's holiday pageant.

101. (d) A New Testament Bible. Anne writes in her diary on November 3, 1943, that her father is giving her a children's Bible so she can find out something about the New Testament. Her sister Margot is perturbed by this Hanukkah gift, so her father decides St. Nicholas Day is a more suitable occasion. "Jesus just doesn't go with Hanukkah," he said.

102. (c) A crossword puzzle book. Anne erases the answers from one of Margot's old puzzle books and suggests that if she waits awhile and forgets, she can do them all over again. Anne knits a scarf in the dark each night after bedtime for her father. She makes the shampoo from the ends of soap mixed with the last of her toilet water and gives it to Mrs. Van Daan. The earplugs, which she makes from cotton and candle wax, are for Mr. Dussel, the dentist. Anne shares a room with the dentist and gives him the earplugs so he isn't disturbed by her fidgeting at night.

103. (b) Lord Allenby, a British military leader, led the British forces in Egypt and Palestine and often combined forces with the army of Maj. T. E. Lawrence, known as "Lawrence of Arabia." Marcus was a United States Army war hero in World War II who died fighting in the Israeli War of Independence. Kirk Douglas portrayed him in *Cast a Giant Shadow.*

104. (c) Lala is decorating a Christmas tree with a star. Peachy enters and admires her Hanukkah bush. Alfred Uhry, author of *Driving Miss Daisy,* wrote *The Last Night of Ballyhoo.*

105. Judith

106. Never. The Hebrew calendar cycles with the moon, so the first day of the month will coincide with the new moon. Hanukkah falls on the 25th day of the month of Kislev, which is long past the new moon.

107. The first three letters spell *Chanu,* which is Hebrew for "they rested." The next two letters stand for numerals: 20 + 5 = 25. Together, the letters mean that on the 25th day of Kislev, they rested from their enemies.

108. (a) Rabbi Joe Black. The rabbi, also a singer and songwriter, wrote "Aleph Bet Boogie." Isaac Stern was a renowned violinist; Ernest Bloch composed music for the synagogue service; Saul Tschernichovsky was a physician who gained fame as a Hebrew poet.

109. (c) Gefilte Joe and the Fish. The group also recorded "I'm a Matzoh, Matzo Man" to the tune of "Macho Man" by the Village People. Rabbi Waxman plays the guitar at B'Nai Israel Congregation in Wilmington, N. C. Melvin Kaminsky is better known as Mel Brooks.

110. (d) Kenny G. The album was *Miracles, The Holiday Album,* which reached the top of the charts in 1994. It was the first holiday album to be at the top of the charts since Mitch Miller claimed the honor thirty-three years earlier.

111. (c) In three flavors —"Raspberry, strawberry, chocolate, too— Those *soufganiot* are so good for you," sings Rabbi Joe Black in the song.

112. (d) The Empire State Building in New York City. Nine-year-old Mallory Greitzer petitioned the building's management for the lights in 1996 but was turned down. The young girl appealed to owner Leona Helmsley, who turned on the blue and white lights in 1997.

113. A Hanukkah Hoedown at Rocky Top Ranch in Keller, Texas, near Dallas featured latkes with beans and franks, the story of Hanukkah told around a blazing campfire, and hayrides for children.

114. (c) In the cemetery. It was a festive occasion at the grave of Altele, the little girl who had been blowing out the Hanukkah candles. The story is told in Isaac Bashevis Singer's collection of Hanukkah tales, *The Power of Light*. Singer, the author of *Yentl, Satan in Goray,* and other titles, has won the Nobel Prize for literature.

115. (c) A yellow-green parakeet in "A Parakeet Named Dreidel." Dreidel was the matchmaker for David and Zelda.

116. (a) Playing dreidel with Falik's children. The mysterious guest lost a thousand *gulden*.

117. (c) The Vatican. Acting on behalf of Pope John Paul, Cardinal Edward Cassidy lit a menorah for the first time in the Vatican in a garden next to an olive tree. The tree was planted to mark the opening of diplomatic ties between Israel and the Vatican. Israel's ambassador to the Holy See, Aharon Lopez, said, "This is an important chapter in the historic process of reconciliation."

118. (d) It was built to celebrate the sack of Jerusalem in A.D. 70. Friezes on the arch depict the Jews being taken into slavery with their holy tablets and candelabra in their arms. Many Roman Jews avoid walking under the arch because it symbolizes ancient enslavement.

119. (c) Israel's fiftieth anniversary

120. Purim and Hanukkah are rabbinical holidays, which are sanctioned by rabbinical action rather than biblical commandment.

121. (b) Herman Wouk, the author of *The Winds of War, War and Remembrance, The Caine Mutiny, Marjorie Morningstar*, and other novels.

122. (d) All of the above. Sandler recalls, "When I was a kid, people would say stupid things to me about my religion. I did that song for other kids, so they could relax a little bit more about not celebrating Christmas. My dad would talk about Kirk Douglas and tell me he's Jewish. I'd say that's good. I didn't feel so alone." Capt. Kirk is William Shatner; Spock is Leonard Nimoy.

123. A menorah sculpted of crystal and bronze, inspired by Jerusalem's Western Wall. It retailed for $725. Waterford marketed a crystal candleholder to mark the eight nights of Hanukkah. Limoges produced hand-painted porcelain dreidels.

124. A yellow UFO rocket–shaped dreidel

125. (c) 1978, Jimmy Carter. It was during the Iran hostage crisis.

126. (a) Jerusalem, at Latrun near the main Jerusalem–Tel Aviv Highway in Israel. The menorah is more than twenty meters tall; it weighs more than seventeen metric tons and spans six hundred square feet. Each night, a cherry picker lifts a rabbi into the air to light its candles.

127. (b) Modi'in, Israel. Torchbearers each year run the thirty-kilometer distance from Modi'in, site of the Maccabean victory, to Jerusalem on the first night of Hanukkah. There is also a reconstructed Maccabean village in Modi'in that is open to the public.

128. (d) Silk lingerie. Phyllis Geronomous buys the lingerie for her trousseau to make her look a young sixty instead of an old sixty-nine.

129. At Niagara Falls, there are menorahs on each side of the falls. The menorahs were first kindled there in 1996.

130. (c) A hut where kids can meet a costumed Judas Maccabee. The hut is an educational project of Chabad Lubavitch. In 1998 the Dreidel House in New Brunswick, New Jersey, hosted six thousand children, who heard the story of the Hanukkah miracle and received chocolate *gelt*.

131. (a) An international Jewish Olympics event that has been held in Israel every four years since 1932. It is the outgrowth of the World Maccabi Union, a worldwide sports organization dedicated to physical fitness. During Hanukkah in 1974 at a relay race sponsored by Maccabi, a torch was carried to an El Al airplane at Lod Airport, then transported to New York City, where an American member of the organization used it to light an American Hanukkah lamp. The torch was extinguished on the airplane.

132. (b) Thirty-six. "Derivation 36/8" is a linear menorah in the Jewish Museum in New York City with thirty-six candle receptacles, each to be filled only once during Hanukkah. Harley Swedler designed the stainless steel-and-aluminum menorah. The text on its backplate, an interpretation of Isaiah 55:13, reads, "In place of the thorn shall come up the cypress."

133. (c) Raoul Wallenberg's family. Wallenberg is the late Swedish diplomat who orchestrated the escape of thousands of Hungarian Jews during the Holocaust.

134. (c) George Washington. According to the story, Washington chanced upon a Polish soldier lighting his Hanukkah lamps during the terrible winter at Valley Forge. The soldier explained how the lamps commemorated the victory of the few over the many. The story so inspired Washington that several years later he located the soldier and presented him with a gold coin engraved with a Hanukkah menorah.

135. (b) Set fire to the dolls

136. On this night most of the candles are lit, signifying light prevailing over darkness.

137. (c) A menorah. The boy can't stand the thought of his father and the other Jewish soldiers not being able to light the menorah and enjoy Hanukkah.

138. (a) Bundles up to see the Hanukkah lights in her neighborhood.

139. (a) The story of Hannah and her seven sons

140. (a) Howard Fast.

141. (c) Chaim Potok recalls a childhood Hanukkah when "darkness almost overpowered the light." It was the first week of November and the final years of the Depression in New York. Radio broadcasts told horrible news of a young Jewish boy who wanted to kill the German ambassador so the world would know about the suffering of Germany's Jews. The boy made a mistake and shot a subordinate instead. Many Jews paid dearly for this in Germany.

   To bring back the meaning of the miracle of Hanukkah, Potok's father lit the last candle on their menorah and proclaimed their family would "give the world the special gifts of our Jewishness, and make their own miracles for the broken planet they live on."

142. (d) There are none. Hanukkah is the sole Jewish festival Anne writes about in her diary.

143. (b) Denim. Rockland's overstuffed dreidel made out of old blue denim work clothes measures twenty-six inches from its point to the top of the handle and can be used as a hassock or cushion.

144. (d) Eight plastic Statue of Liberty candleholders stand on a base wrapped in an American-flag design.

145. (c) Emma Lazarus's poem, "The New Colossus." The last six lines of the poem are printed on the bottom of the menorah. "The New Colossus" appears on the base of the actual Statue of Liberty.

146. (c) Doodle Dreidel came with a marking pen tip that created art as it spun across a piece of paper.

147. (a) Ancient Maccabean coins

148. (b) Bezalel; it was made of pure gold with seven cups shaped like almond blossoms.

149. (d) All of the above.

150. (d) He is a translator of William Shakespeare's works.

151. (c) Menorahs. The museum has 1,150 menorahs in its collection, with 40 on view at all times. The viewing total goes up to 60 during the Hanukkah season. A menorah of interest is an Australian one made from a Victorian souvenir, adorned with kangaroos and emus.

152. (b) Dr. Hannibal Lechter, in the book *Hannibal*. Dr. Lechter is the cannibalistic mad scientist played by Anthony Hopkins in *The Silence of The Lambs*.